*This book is dedicated to all those who have ever been hurt.*

# Forgiveness is the Key

## 12 Steps for Letting Go and Reclaiming Your Life

### Nicole Bayliss

FORGIVENESS IS THE KEY

First published in 2021 by Dragonfly Publications.

Copyright © Nicole Bayliss, 2021

All rights reserved. The moral rights of the author have been asserted under *Copyright Amendment (Moral Rights) Act 2000*.

Except as permitted under the Australian *Copyright Act 1968* (for example, a fair dealing for the purposes of study, research, criticism or review), no part of this book may be reproduced, stored in a retrieval system, communicated or transmitted in any form or by any means without prior written permission.

ISBN: 978-0-6452936-1-6

Printed by Lightning Source.
Cover Design and Layout: Ben Crompton Design

For information on ordering further copies of the book or to contact the author please visit nicolebayliss.com.au

# Contents

Introduction ..... 9
1. Forgiveness starts with acceptance ..... 15
2. Forgiving is not condoning ..... 21
3. Be willing to forgive ..... 25
4. Self-righteousness is your enemy ..... 29
5. Forgiveness is letting go ..... 33
6. Forgiveness isn't about staying or dropping your boundaries ..... 37
7. Choose not to take it personally ..... 41
8. Soothe your wounded self ..... 47
9. Look deeper into the other side of the story ..... 51

10. Take responsibility for your part if needed — 55

11. Be willing to learn the lesson — 61

12. Forgive yourself — 65

Conclusion — 71

About the Author — 73

*We all agree that forgiveness is a beautiful idea*
*Until we have to practise it.*

**C.S. Lewis**

# Introduction

**Why forgive?**

Life is such that along the way we all get hurt, disappointed, betrayed or let down at some point. Some of us get a worse deal than others, but none of us get through life without being hurt.

It is not what happens to us that really harms us however; it is what we do or do not do about it that harms us.

Forgiving can be an extremely difficult thing to do. Not forgiving can give us a sense of strength and protection, and yet all it does is close off our heart and harden us. Hanging onto old pain and feelings of anger and resentment are harmful to our health and wellbeing, and keeps us in a low vibration which draws to us even more low vibrational experiences.

Do not underestimate the power of forgiveness! It is a key element to our being able to manifest and enjoy love, wellness, abundance and success.

Whomever and whatever we do not forgive stays with us karmically. Even if we leave people or situations that have hurt us, we will be sent more of the same unless we forgive the "original sin." In other words, until we forgive, our lives will remain blocked in one way or another.

Unforgiveness keeps us stuck and unable to expand into evermore love and abundance, while forgiveness frees us, clears our karmic slate and opens us up for greater and better things.

This little book is easy to read and provides

a simple process so that you CAN forgive and release all that may be blocking you from moving forward in love and peace.

You deserve to live your best life. You deserve to feel light and free.

Namaste,

Nicole x

*We must develop and maintain the capacity to forgive.*
*He who is devoid of the power to forgive*
*Is devoid of the power to love.*

**Martin Luther King**

# 1. Forgiveness starts with acceptance

Forgiveness must begin with acceptance.

1. Acceptance that the event happened
2. Acceptance of how you truly feel about it
3. Acceptance of yourself
4. Acceptance that the other person is who they are.

Let's explore these four points.

**Acceptance that the event happened**

It is normal to struggle with accepting that something happened that we didn't want to happen, or that we couldn't foresee would happen. And yet there are no accidents in life. All is as it should be. It can be difficult to accept that life can hand you a painful experience, however you are here to transform and grow, and you only transform and grow through challenges, not through everything going your way.

The Buddhists tell us that life is a series of "dis-illusionment". One by one, the veils of illusion are removed so that we see life more clearly. Of course this can be extremely painful, but when we accept that everything really does happen for a reason - even if we do not know right now what that reason is - the pain of resistance will be removed.

## Acceptance of how you truly feel about it

Many of us have been taught not to feel or show our "negative" feelings. We can even feel ashamed of how we really feel, and yet the most healthy thing you can do when you have been hurt is to accept and feel your feelings.

It is normal to feel hurt, sad, angry, betrayed, resentful, and even vengeful. You do not have to act on these feelings, but you certainly have the right to feel your feelings, because they are your truth in the present moment. Every feeling needs to felt and acknowledged. This is how feelings get naturally processed.

## Acceptance of yourself

Allowing yourself to feel what you truly feel is an act of self-love and self-acceptance. You are the most important person in your life. You deserve your own love more than anyone else. By lovingly accepting how you feel, you give yourself permission to be you, and you create a space where you can nurture yourself. Lovingly telling yourself that you have the right to feel how you feel is powerful.

## Acceptance that the other person is who they are

It can be a struggle to accept that the other person is who they are and that they did what they did. But remember the veils of dis-illusionment. In any relationship, we eventually get shown many aspects of a person. We can get stuck in trying to figure out "Why would they do that?" or "How could they do that?"

We can get stuck in our own judgement of the person, instead of accepting the truth about that person without judgment. We can choose to accept that all people have both their positive and negative aspects, and in this particular instance you can choose to accept that you have been shown a negative aspect of that person.

*Acceptance of what has happened is the first step in overcoming any misfortune.*

**William James**

# 2. Forgiving is not condoning

It's a common belief that if we forgive, we are indicating that we are OK with what happened. This is NOT true!

You don't need to condone, agree with or approve of what the other person did in order to forgive them. This is what holds many people back from forgiving. You have the right to:

1. Feel the way you feel

2. Disagree and disapprove of what the other person did

3. Dislike what the other person did.

And yet you can still forgive!

*Forgiveness doesn't make the other person right;
It makes YOU free.*

**Stormie Omartian**

# 3. Be willing to forgive

To forgive, we must be willing. We become willing when we realise that holding onto the pain and negative karma created by unforgiveness is harming us, and not the other person. Forgiveness is an act of self love!

You are worthy of living your best life. You are worthy of feeling light, free and joyful. If you are willing to feel free, you are willing to forgive.

If you are willing to forgive, declare:

*I am willing to forgive!*

*Forgiveness is not always easy.*
*At times it feels more painful than the wound we suffered,*
*To forgive the one that inflicted it.*
*And yet, there is no peace without forgiveness.*
*Attack thoughts towards others are attack thoughts towards ourselves.*
*The first step in forgiveness is the willingness to forgive.*

**Marianne Williamson**

# 4. Self-righteousness is your enemy

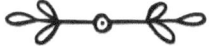

The energy of self-righteousness can be addictive. Self-righteousness comes from the part of yourself that feels victimised and powerless. From this place, you become attached to the story of "being wronged".

It can feel good and even powerful to feel self-righteous, but self-righteousness gets you nowhere except stuck in the story of what happened and stuck in the "poor me" of the victim. Self-righteousness can look and feel like power, but it's actually the opposite.

Being willing to let go of self-righteousness can feel frightening, because it can become a strong part of our identity. If we let go of our self-righteousness, then who will we be?

Self-righteousness comes from the ego that believes in "right" and "wrong". If you have a strong sense of "right" and "wrong", then letting go of self-righteousness can be difficult, because if you let go of the idea that the other person wasn't "wrong", then you're faced with the idea that maybe you aren't "right".

In order to let go of self-righteousness, we need to rise above the concept of "right" and "wrong" and ascend to the place of "just is".

To move out of self-righteousness, declare:

*I now let go of all self-righteousness.*

*Those who cannot forgive others*
*Break the bridge over which they themselves must pass.*

**Confucius**

# 5. Forgiveness is letting go

Forgiveness is choosing to let go of the toxic emotions such as anger, resentment and vengeance that harm YOU, not the other person. Once you have felt and acknowledged these emotions, make a conscious choice to let them go.

You can declare:

*I acknowledge that I feel (name your feelings) and I now choose to let these feelings go.*

You may need to do this every day for a while, because healing is a process. Our wounded self attempts to hold onto these feelings in the misguided notion that we are protecting ourselves by staying hurt and angry.

There is no need to denigrate yourself if difficult feelings remain with you for a time. Simply acknowledge them, feel them and choose to let them go. Be kind to yourself during your forgiveness process.

*When we hate our enemies, we are giving them power over us;*
*Power over our sleep, our appetites,*
*our blood pressure, our health and our happiness.*
*Our enemies would dance with joy if only they knew*
*How they were worrying us, lacerating us,*
*And getting even with us!*
*Our hate is not hurting them at all,*
*But our hate is turning our days and nights*
*Into a hellish turmoil.*

**Dale Carnegie**

# 6. Forgiveness isn't about staying or dropping your boundaries

Forgiveness does not mean that we open up and become vulnerable once again to the person who hurt us. Forgiveness does not require that we stay in a relationship with the person, or allow our relationship with that person to go back to the way it was. In some cases, it is better to end a relationship with the person who hurt us than to continue it. Some people are not worthy of having a place in our lives. In other cases, we may allow that person to be in our lives, but on new terms.

The incident that required our forgiveness may have taken away a veil of illusion that we had about that person. We see the person more realistically now. From this new vision must come decisions for our highest good. If it no longer feels self-honouring to have a relationship with this person, we must honour our own truth.

If we choose to continue a relationship with this person, we may need to adjust the boundaries to protect ourselves from being hurt again.

Having healthy boundaries means not allowing anyone to compromise our values and our choices.

Loving, honouring and respecting ourselves must come before our relationship with anybody else. The love we have for ourselves is the solid foundation through which we create all our relationships.

*Forgiveness is not about forgetting;*
*It is letting go of another person's throat.*

**William P. Young**

# 7. Choose not to take it personally

Being hurt, let down or betrayed can feel like a dagger being driven through your heart. The pain can be great, and it is made greater than it needs to be because we take it personally.

Yes, that person may have deliberately set out to hurt you, to con you, to abuse you, to use you or to disappoint you. Why wouldn't you take it personally? Of course you would! We all do!

And yet if we were to stand back from it all, we would probably see that this person wouldn't do what they did just to us. They would probably do it to anyone in the same circumstances. In this instance, it just so happened to be you.

Wherever we go in life, we take ourselves with us. I have witnessed people doing the same thing over and over to different people, because they have not dealt with the issue underlying their own behaviour.

I have seen people move from one relationship to another, taking themselves with them and repeating hurts and betrayals.

Do not fool yourself that it's only you who will ever be hurt by this person. We can all move on physically to pastures new, but we still take ourselves with us.

Unless a person is willing to take ownership of their behaviours and commit to changing them, they will continue to be who they are and do what they do.

Knowing this, we can release ourselves from the inner torture of taking it all so personally.

When we choose to not take the incident personally, our pain lessens, and we realise that we can soothe and heal ourselves.

- Forgiveness is the Key -

*Not taking things personally
Is a true sign of maturity.*

**Robert Celner**

# 8. Soothe your wounded self

Our wounded self has no time for anybody else's pain except his or her own. When we've been wounded, the pain can be overwhelming. This isn't our fault; trauma does this. However your wounded self is not the only part of you.

You also have a kind and compassionate adult that dwells within you, and you can access him or her to comfort your wounded self. Be the kind and caring friend or parent to your wounded self that they long for. Talk to your wounded self and reassure them. Here are some suggestions:

- I love you and I am here for you.
- I know you're hurting.

- I'll never leave you.
- It's ok; I'm here.
- Together, we're going to be OK.

To self-soothe is to self-love. Learn to do this regularly, and you will find that you become stronger and more courageous.

*Sometimes I wish that I could go into a time machine right now
And just look at myself and say "Calm down. Things are gonna be fine.
Things are gonna be all great. Just relax."*

**Tristan Wilds**

# 9. Look deeper into the other side of the story

When we look deeper into the "other side of the story", we are able to get a clearer perspective of why things happened as they did. Ponder the following question about the person who hurt you:

*What happened to you to make you want to do this?*

Wounded children can grow up to wound others. Abused children may grow up to abuse others.

You can visualise the person who hurt you as a child, and ask the question again.

*What happened to you?*

You may get realisations. You may even feel a sense of compassion for the other person.

In any case, you will broaden your perspective beyond the immediate story of persecutor and victim.

*Wounded people wound people.*

**Anonymous**

# 10. Take responsibility for your part if needed

Taking responsibility for our part is not applicable to anything that happened to us in childhood, because as children we did not choose the circumstances that we were in. As children, we are at the mercy of our caregivers. We do not have the right to choose what happens to us as children. So if you are reading this book so as to heal childhood trauma, this page is not applicable to you.

If however, you are seeking to forgive something that happened to you as an adult, this page is highly important for your forgiveness process. As adults we do have choices, and sometimes we make mistakes. There is nothing wrong with making a mistake as long as we take responsibility and learn from that mistake. Life is a school and we are here to learn, and sometimes we make mistakes so as to learn a valuable lesson. When we learn the lesson, we grow and take the learning with us into the future.

As adults, we must not fall into the trap of believing that we were simply in the "wrong place at the wrong time". This is "victim thinking" and will keep us repeating a negative situation over and over again until we take responsibility and learn the lesson.

Everything happens for a reason, even the adult trauma you went through. Every relationship is 50/50.

- You cannot have a persecutor without a victim.
- You cannot have an abuser without someone who is willing on some level to be abused.
- You cannot have a conman or conwoman

without someone who is willing on some level to be conned.

To take responsibility for your part, declare:

*I am willing to take responsibility for my part in this.*

Sometimes we may not be aware of what it is within us that attracted a negative situation because much of what is in our energy field is not conscious yet. It is not your fault!

You didn't deliberately go about seeking someone to abuse you or rob you or harm you. Taking responsibility does not mean blaming ourselves.

*When you think everything
Is someone else's fault
You suffer a lot.
When you realise everything springs
Only from yourself,
You will learn by peace and joy.*

**His Holiness The Dalai Lama**

# 11. Be willing to learn the lesson

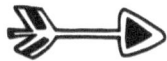

Our energy field contains old family and ancestral patterns and self-limiting beliefs that can attract us to people and situations that mirror back to us something that needs to be addressed and healed. And so you can declare:

*Even though I don't know why I attracted this situation into my life, I am willing to learn the necessary lessons for my highest good.*

Do not be concerned whether or not the other person takes in their lessons; that is their business and not yours. Your business is to take in the important lessons from this hurtful and negative experience. You can do this by asking yourself the following questions (some of these questions may not apply to all situations - choose the ones that do apply):

- *Did I have any early warning bells that I ignored?*
- *If so, why did I ignore them?*
- *Did I choose actions that didn't serve me?*
- *In what ways did I betray myself?*
- *What did I want from this person?*
- *How can I give that to myself?*
- *What would I do differently next time?*

By doing this, you are choosing to GROW from this situation, rather than staying stuck in victim consciousness.

When you choose to learn the lessons, and take these valuable lessons with you into the future, you will create a new transformed reality.

*Your mistakes are a part of being human.*
*Appreciate your mistakes for what they are:*
*Precious life lessons that can only be learned the hard way.*
*Unless it's a fatal mistake,*
*which, at least, others can learn from.*

**Al Franken**

# 12. Forgive yourself

*Love*

Nothing is more torturous nor punishing than not forgiving yourself. Not being able to forgive yourself can lead to:

- Self-hatred
- Self-criticism
- Self-judgment
- Self punishment
- Self-sabotage.
- Depression
- Illness.

These are very good reasons to begin the process of self-forgiveness. Your relationship with yourself is the most important relationship you will ever have.

Begin by asking yourself:

*What do I need to forgive myself for?*

Write it all down - get it out of your system! And then declare:

*I am willing to forgive myself for (name it).*

Do this for everything you need to forgive yourself for.

Meet yourself with kindness and compassion. Everybody makes mistakes. We have all done things or thought things that we feel ashamed of.

Every mistake was inevitable with the knowledge and level of awareness we had at the time.

Be kind to yourself as you embrace the process of self-forgiveness. It may take a little time, but trust in the process.

You, more than anyone deserve your own forgiveness.

*Never forget that to forgive yourself*
*Is to release trapped energy*
*That could be doing good work in the world.*

**D. Patrick Miller**

# Conclusion

**The miracle of forgiveness**

Through forgiveness we clear our own karmic slate and attract in more positive and loving experiences, instead of repeating negative patterns.

There are many studies that have shown forgiveness has a positive effect on mental and physical health.

Forgiveness creates miracles, and it is imperative if we are to heal and live our best lives.

Namaste.

Nicole x

# **About the Author**

Nicole is an author, spiritual teacher and healer who is based in Sydney, Australia.

Nicole works with people all over the world, facilitating personal transformation.

She has written five other books, A Shift to Bliss, 5 Steps to Finding Love, Soul Magic, Soulful & Successful Business and The 25 Universal Laws.

Nicole offers free meditations on the app Insight Timer and her online courses are [available from her website](available from her website).